Center for Basque Studies
Basque Literature Series, No. 6

BASQUE LITERATURE SERIES

BERNARDO ATXAGA

Two Basque Stories

Translated from Basque by
Nere Lete

Basque Literature Series Editor
Mari Jose Olaziregi

Center for Basque Studies
University of Nevada, Reno

Center for Basque Studies
Basque Literature Series, No. 6

Center for Basque Studies
University of Nevada, Reno
Reno, Nevada 89557
http://basque.unr.edu

Basque Literature Series Editor: Mari Jose Olaziregi

Series design © 2009 by Jose Luis Agote.
Drawings by Antton Olariaga.
Cover design by Jose Luis Agote, with a drawing by A. Olariaga.

Library of Congress Cataloging-in-Publication Data

Atxaga, Bernardo.
[Short stories. English. Selections]
Two Basque stories / Bernardo Atxaga ; translated from Basque by
Nere Lete.
    p. cm. -- (Basque literature series ; no. 6)
"Originally published as Bi letter jaso nituen oso denbora gutxian
and Sugeak txoriari begiratzen dionean by Erein (Basque Country-
Spain), c1984"--T.p. verso.
ISBN 978-1-877802-85-0 (pbk. : alk. paper)
1. Atxaga, Bernardo--Translations into English. I. Lete, Nere.
II. Atxaga, Bernardo. Bi letter jaso nituen oso denbora gutxian.
English. III. Atxaga, Bernardo. Sugeak txoria'ri begiratzen dionean.
English. IV. Title.
PH5339.A8A2 2009
899'.923--dc22
                                        2009034647

Acknowledgments

The Center for Basque Studies wishes to gratefully acknowledge the generous financial support of the Government of the Basque Autonomous Community for the publication of this book.

BERNARDO ATXAGA

Two Letters All at Once

I received two letters all at once, within ten days of each other. Both came directly to the house I have here in this American *hiri* of Boise, and my grandson Jimmy handed them to me. When he came with the last one, I was trimming the branches of the mimosa tree, in good spirits, certainly, because when I'm in a bad mood I don't feel like working in the garden, and I gave him a dollar as a reward. But Jimmy was staring at me with that cute ways of his, puckering up his nose as if worried.

"What, Jimmy?" I asked him, "Isn't that enough, *txo-txo*?"

"No, it's not that, *aitite*," he answered, grabbing the stamp I gave him for his collection.

"Then, what?"

"Why do you get so many letters from Europe, *aitite*?" he asked me with that fine English they teach him at the *eskola*. I tried to explain it to him the best I could, in my not-so-good English. What else could I do? You can't teach an old dog new tricks. I told him that I was from somewhere in Europe . . . that I still had some family there . . . that I also had friends and . . . that that was the reason I received some letters from the other side of the ocean. Of course I would have liked to give Jimmy more details, and to say to him: "Don't think, *txo-txo*, that I get so many letters. The ones you brought me were the first ones in three long years!" But no way. That's more words than my not so-good-English could handle. Yes, it's a shame not to be able to tell my stories to Jimmy. I can't explain to him where I'm from. I can't explain where his last name, *Agirre*, comes from. What a nice last name, *Agirre, polita benetan*. I can't even explain that. What a great shame. But you don't learn anything in the mountains, surely not English. The mountains are cruel, and I spent almost forty years up there— what am I saying, forty! It was sixty, sixty years, imagine, always herding sheep, always completely alone, and now what? Damn it!

It happens to all of us, to all the sheepherders who have lived in the mountains. Don't think I am any dumber than the rest. Once a year the Governor of Idaho used to come to ask us how we were doing; he used to come to the sheepherders' ball we had every year.

"OK, Mister Governor," we all would answer. Because "OK" was the only thing we knew how to say. That's what we sheepherders are: just plain ignorant. All of us used to "understand" some English, thanks to the radio, because we were always listening to it. Anything else, forget it. And now that I'm an old man, I can't explain things to my *txo-txo*.

Besides, at first I'd planned to go back to my hometown, I wanted to see my country before I died. That was also why I didn't even try with this English. The home fire was pulling at me and I felt like going

back. But in the meantime, my sons were growing up, and they had made friends here, and finally married women from here. That was it. I decided to stay here as an American, with all its disadvantages, of course, but I decided to stay. Yes, sir; *bai, jauna.* And to tell the truth, I don't regret it at all, no, sir! *Ez, jauna!* What did I have while I lived in my own village? Really, nothing. Boiled potatoes and beans to eat. Some rags that here not even the most down-and-out *eskale* at the Rescue Mission would wear. And old *alpargatak* for my feet. Money, what was that? It was miserable there. Now at least I own my own home, a house with a *lorategi* and everything, where I have my mimosa trees, my roses, and even a couple of cypress trees. That's how I live now, taking care of the *lorategi* and going for walks, with no fear of the future. Perhaps it's not a lot, but I'm satisfied. There are many with less than that.

The thing is that I didn't go back to my town. It was enough to have a *postetxe* close by. Twice a year or so one of my relatives back home would write me a few words and I was satisfied with that. But little by little the mail stopped coming; my brother died, then my sister. Both of them were quite elderly, and as the old saying goes, "Among the young, only a few will die, but among the old, everyone." I'm old too, I'll be eighty soon, but I'm pretty stubborn and I am not looking forward to leaving this world. Besides, from the time I was young I've had a thing about outliving all my friends. When I lost my brothers and sisters, I

asked myself, what about those two friends of mine? Can they still be alive?

Someone might think that was a stupid thing, but it bothered me. What had happened to my friends, Beltza, the dark-haired one, and skinny Iharra? But now, even that doubt is gone. Those two letters that came, one after another, brought my friends' funeral cards. A bad cold took Iharra, that's what his widow writes me. What backward ways. Here in America a cold doesn't wipe out anyone. Beltza, on the other hand, fell down the stairs. That's what his daughter says in a very long letter. Tough luck. It could happen to anyone. Things like that happen here, too. But, as his daughter says, no one can change God's will. That Beltza's girl must really be a gossip. She wrote me so many things in her letter, and I appreciate it. That way, an old guy like me is entertained and doesn't get bored.

That's the worst thing about turning eighty. You get bored, you always have too much free time. At least that's what has happened to me. I work in the *lorategi*, I stay at home, I fight with my daughter-in-law because she has Irish blood, and Irish people are even more stubborn than we Basques. I go to pick up Jimmy, and then I still have so much time left before I go to bed. So, I start thinking, what else is there to do? I won't stare at that television, I only watch football and other sports, and those cartoons, too. But other than that, I don't watch anything. I don't like it at all, and besides, I don't understand half of what goes on. That's why I start thinking, because what else can I do? It's become such a habit. Naturally, sheepherders think a lot. All those hours alone, that's why.

So, I started thinking about those two letters. At first, over and over again I thought that they would be the last ones.

Old Martin, that's what everybody calls me here. Old Martin, I thought to myself, from now on you're history in your town. The stories have all ended. Man, no one you know is left. If you would've sent something to your town as others did, some money, a big reputation, some kind of gift or other, you would've gotten a Christmas card at least. But, man, since you never sent anything, now to hell with you, Old Martin. You haven't become a big shot in the States, but you have had some extra money, at least enough to send some over there. Especially with what dollars are worth here. But you've always been so tight, so greedy, so fond of money—Old Martin, the cheapskate.

That's a funny thing, too. I mean, to start talking to yourself and even scolding yourself. But what can you do in those situations? You can't blame it on anyone else. People have to listen to their conscience, especially when it's right. And in my case it's right, I've always loved money, *bai, jauna.* No use denying it. I've never stolen anything in my entire life, I've lived an honest life so I can be saved when my last judgment day comes. *Ez, jauna,* Old Martin has never stolen anything.

But back to what I was saying. I thought a lot about those letters and I kept them in my pocket for a long time. Whenever I was bored, I pulled them out and read them, especially the one from Beltza's daughter, since, like I said, it had more meat. There I was, reading and reading, hoping that it would stir up my darn memory. That's another thing, I have a very bad memory; I don't remember half of what has happened to me.

It's really amazing how bad my memory is. Kathleen, that Irish daughter-in-law of mine, doesn't want to believe me. She says that it is not a question of ability but of will; that I don't want to tell anything about my life; in that way I am like a criminal. Kathleen, on the other hand, knows every little corner of Ireland by heart, even though she left there when she was a child. She knows her homeland from what her father told her.

"And how do you know whether that father of yours told you the truth or not?"

Sure, let's say they tell me that foxes in Ireland are green, I have no choice but to believe it. I'm not going over there to check it out.

"There are books, Old Martin, there are books!" she tells me, tilting her head to one side, showing off her bright red hair, because it falls in her face when she moves that way. She treats me as if I were a dummy. But Old Martin is not one to keep quiet.

"And just how do you figure out if those books are telling the truth or not? Huh? How do you figure that out?"

And then, what comes next is inevitable. First, she tells my son that it's impossible to argue with me.

Then, in half an hour or so, she reminds me that I can't eat sweets.

"You know what the doctor told you, *aitite.*"

With that, she takes the chocolate pudding away from me, something she doesn't do when I don't interrupt her father's stories. That's her revenge. And people talk about justice. Baloney! When it suits her, pudding for *aitite,* when it doesn't, no pudding. When she is going to the movies and has no choice but to leave Jimmy with me, pudding for *aitite,* but when I attack that saintly father of hers, no pudding. It's hell to be old, you end up under the thumb of a moody woman. And besides, I'm not sick at all, I just shouldn't eat sweets. I'm not very lucky in that way. I go to the doctor and what does he tell me? No sweets, *gozorik ez!* And I am crazy about chocolate pudding.

But let's put aside this family mess and get back to my bad memory. As I said before, I was always carrying the letters in my jacket pocket, hoping they would help me remember. A trip to the drugstore? I would sit in a corner and read them. Going to pick up Jimmy? There I was with my letters. My daughter-in-law tried to make fun of me about that, too, saying that people would say, "Is Old Martin fooling around or what? He is always reading those letters." But I don't keep quiet, I defend myself even with my mediocre English; but as I already said, they can say whatever they want. Besides, what the hell, I am still in good shape.

Kathleen cracks up when I say that. And I tell her: "Go ahead and laugh, woman. Why don't you bring that sister of yours over, the old maid, and leave her in my room? Then you would see some action in this place!"

"What do you mean, action?" poor Jimmy chimes in. He is only eight, and doesn't know about those things.

"*Aitite* says that he wants to have a baby with your aunt. What do you think, Jimmy?"

"That's great, mom!" says Jimmy. Poor Jimmy, *gixajoa*. I'm always telling them that the boy is pretty lonely at home all by himself, that he needs a brother or a sister. And look, *gixajoa,* he thinks whatever his mother says is great.

"But," teases his mother, "what do you think? Is *aitite* still in shape to do 'dzast'?"

"Dzast?" asks the poor kid.

"Let's go trim the mimosa with the clippers, Jimmy!" I say, so things don't get out of hand. I tell Kathleen, I tell her not to mention those things to the boy, but it's no use. Those Irish people are pretty crude about those things. Very crude. When it's bath time, they take baths together, mom, dad, and Jimmy, the three of them stark naked. At first they also asked me to take a bath, naked, with the boy. Me, taking a bath with the kid, bare naked? That's all I needed. There's respect for you! "I'm not out of my mind," I told them, shaking my cane, "I'm not out of my mind, *ezta erotuta ere!* You might be shameless, but not me!"

Thank God, thank God I kept at it. Otherwise, who knows what that hardheaded Kathleen would have asked me to do next.

But I've lost track again. I was obsessed with those letters, that's what I was saying, completely obsessed. Sometimes you imagine someone is watching you, it's a feeling, and you look back over your shoulder and, wham, it's true. And I had a similar feeling, that there was something in those letters, a mystery or something I couldn't get ahold of. And, sure enough, there was. Finally, after reading them over and over, finally Old Martin got it, and started remembering many things. That's how it happened.

The letter that Beltza's gabby daughter had written really puzzled me. As I said before, she told me about all the town gossip, but she was hiding something from me. Actually, it was the only thing I did know that happened in my town. Beltza's daughter didn't mention anything about Iharra's death.

How come she doesn't tell me anything about it? I asked myself. After all, Iharra had died a few days before her father. Didn't I get both funeral cards at the same time?

And that's how they say memory works. All of a sudden, everything came back to me. Now I knew the reason why she left that out. Beltza and Iharra were mad at each other when they died; after all those years, they were still mad.

As soon as I realized that, I began remembering again. That weak memory started working again, like

when the power comes back on after a storm. A light bulb comes on in one room, the radio in another, the fridge starts humming, and from inside neighbors' houses, squares of light begin to brighten the darkness. Something like that happened to me, too. I said to myself: Old Martin, you better start writing everything you remember down on paper. If not, you may forget it all as you did before, and you will be hunting forever, without being able to get back at Kathleen. Think hard about what happened between Beltza and Iharra and then, make a splash after dinner. Tell your story and see what that Irish one says. See if she is still as arrogant as she is now.

And that is how I started writing down the story of how my two friends got mad at each other, writing very neatly, putting the beginning first and the end last. The three of us, Beltza, Iharra, and I, did everything together in that isolated town. We used to work in the mountains as loggers, we did everything together, young and strong, always eating beans, *babak* at breakfast, *babak* for lunch, *babak* for dinner; *babak* for every single meal. Sometimes we had ham, a little ham lost in the *babak,* but not very often. Our boss used to tell us that *babak* were good for our health. Health? Bull! There wasn't anything else! Weekdays and weekends, we were always together. Every Sunday, after eating all those *babak,* we headed for the bar. We used to spend more than half the afternoon drinking, *zurrutan,* sometimes singing, sometimes arguing, making terrible fun of each other, on and on. As it started to get dark, we would walk

the fifteen steps that separated the bar from the dance
hall; by that time the dance would already be started.
If anyone could see Old Martin now he would prob-
ably say: "Are you saying that this chubby *aitite* used
to dance? Come on, are you kidding me?"

"No way!"

"That's unbelievable!"

They might say that, but they'd be wrong. I was
an excellent dancer, excellent, a great dancer, indeed.
I remembered that before, too, and of course Kathleen refused to believe me, but one Fourth of July, my
son came and brought a record home. I don't know
where the music came from but it was a lot like the
music from back home. I got up from the table and
danced a fandango all the way through. Later, Jimmy
had to fan me with a magazine to give me some air,
because I was out of breath, but we settled the dancing question. Dancing is like everything else, you
have to be born to it, that's all. My father used to say,
"You either are a dancer or you're not. There is no
other choice."

My father was a dancer and so am I. Kathleen had
to admit it. "Wonderful! Wonderful!" she kept saying
while I was dancing. And if that Irish one said that,
just imagine . . .

Because I was such a good dancer, I used to spend
the whole evening dancing with this one or that one
without stopping to rest. All the girls wanted to see
if they could measure up to me, to see if they could
wear me out, and that's how it was, one would come
up, then another, they'd play one song, then another,

and I would be sweating, soaking wet, but without getting tired at all, I wouldn't get tired—everybody else got tired before I did. There was, now I remember, a girl that could keep up with me; she also was a natural dancer, a stout girl, just looking at her you wouldn't think she was so graceful with those chunky legs, but what a way of moving she had when she danced, how she made those shoes fly! She had boys flocking around her like I had girls, she wore them all out. She was tireless. I had completely forgotten about it, but she was like that. And I remember that we never tested each other because we were afraid of each other. Once, during the town's festival, they asked us if we would challenge each other, and we said that we would do it, since it was the festival. And then, when the day came, they brought two accordion players, so they could take turns; so we had no break. We danced for about an hour without stopping even once. Then we quit, since we had planned it that way beforehand. There was a lot of debate in town; people argued which of us was the best.

I was that kind of dancer; Iharra and Beltza, on the other hand, were completely different kinds of guys. They didn't dance. They used to stare in silence, often leaning against a column in the archway.

Beltza was kind of an animal, and he was crazy about girls; he would take a girl and walk her home along the little pathways of that humble town. Don't think he would pick anyone special, no way, *ez horixe*. He had only two things in mind: was the girl easy, and how far away was her house. That's how he operated.

There was one in town, a girl I mean, who after the
first turn in the path, agreed to a little titty-touching.
She lived up in the mountains two hours away from
the bar. Most of the time, Beltza would be hooked up
with her. God knows what Beltza did to her on the
last turn. We never knew, not even the night we followed them. I was very bashful when it came to girl
matters and so was Iharra. I wasn't nearly as good at
those things as I was at dancing, and besides, in those
days you had to be careful; if you accompanied a girl
seven times, and if you touched her a few times, you
were on the verge of marriage. That's if you weren't
an animal. Beltza didn't give a damn about marriage.
Easy women, that's all he cared about. And if the girl
wanted to get married, sure, when hell freezes over!
But to play that game you had to be that way, and
Beltza was.

I didn't want to get married, because by that time
I had already decided to come to America. There I
would be, dancing and carrying on, but I didn't have
any intention of staying there. I wanted to jump
aboard a ship, I was always thinking about it, about
the ship and the money I needed for the passage.
Since I didn't have any good way to make money,
I would dance. And besides I had to work the *babak*
off somehow.

Iharra was made from another mold. A little sad,
but loyal, a good worker. He wasn't good at all with
girls, even worse than me. Even when we would follow Beltza, other guys and me, Iharra's shyness was
famous. He wouldn't go with us, he would stay in

town, as if the girl business frightened him. When Beltza came back, or the day after he was with a girl, Iharra didn't want to listen to the stories, not even if we were in the woods; he would go off to work by himself.

To tell the truth, the stories that Beltza used to tell about those nights were amazing, very crude. Besides, he liked to brag, he used to like to spread the news about his conquests. The further away Iharra would go in the woods, the louder Beltza would shout his stories, to make Iharra more furious.

"I grabbed her from way under here and . . ."

He used to start like that, shouting like I said before; I think the whole town could hear his news.

Beltza was a real rascal. You couldn't joke with him much. Even though he liked to laugh at others, he used to get mad if someone else did the same to him. I think that even the priest was afraid of him. Maybe he would see him, the priest I mean, walking along the path, when we were working on a hillside in the woods, and he would shout, "Where are you going, man? Where are you going, you pig? Once again to eat at someone else's expense?" And, of course, in that humble town of ours surrounded by nothing but mountains and hollows, there are tremendous echoes everywhere, and I am sure that what Beltza told him made its way to every single house. And so, the priest kept quiet, passing by without saying a single word. He must have thought, If I say something, that crazy man is going to do me in. And who knows, who knows what Beltza was capable of.

He was so angry at priests, so angry. Ever since he was little. Because they punished us a lot when we were kids. For doing anything, even the most trivial thing, they would make us kneel in the plaza, all of us kids in a line, more than forty of us, with our knees bleeding from the gravel. That happened many, many times; it was unforgivable. Even I have never forgiven them, and I am more easy-going than Beltza.

Kathleen is surprised because I don't pray much, because, well, those Irish people are worse than we are when it comes to religious matters; they have religion more deeply implanted in them. When I was living in my town, I didn't think so, I thought that such a religious people only existed in backwards towns like mine. But look at Kathleen, she's been in America for almost her entire life and she scolds me because I don't pray enough. But, well, I have to tell her what that priest was like. See what she thinks of the priest, a family could be starving and still be obligated to serve him the best food they had. What a glutton he was! But that wasn't what hurt Beltza the most, what really hurt him was the thing about women. Because, this happened to him a lot, even though the girl was easy, she still wouldn't go along, she was afraid of the confessional, so she wouldn't go along with him. As he used to say, that made it very hard work. And another thing, the priest didn't want anyone dancing close, only fandangos, and even then only until ten o'clock. Beltza liked waltzing a lot so that's why he was so mad.

Winters used to be very hard in that country. Mud everywhere, cold everywhere, and almost nothing to do for fun on Sundays because the accordion players didn't play at that time of the year; they said their hands would freeze, and maybe it was true. So there was nothing left for us but drinking, *zurrutan,* and next day back to the hills.

The mountains are very sad in winter, they are the same as here, anywhere.

You look at one side, and you see a leafless oak grove, as if it were full of skeletons; you look in another direction and you see empty trails, no people, no animals, no nothing, and harsh silence. The nicest thing in winter, in that town of ours at least, used to be the creek. The water would give off steam, as if it were boiling, and that would warm you a little bit.

Often we wouldn't go outside at all, not even to work, and there we would be at home, eating chestnuts, *gaztainak,* and staring at the fire. Sitting in front of the fire made me so bored that I couldn't wait for spring to come, that is, until the day I decided to go to America. Once I made up my mind about that, I enjoyed sitting by the fire, almost more than going out. Fire helps you, because that's the nature of fire, you stare at it and the hours pass by without you realizing it; the more things you have to think about, the easier time passes.

And that's exactly what happened to me: the thought of going to America gave me many things to think about.

When I got a house in this *hiri* of Boise, that was my first project, to put in a fireplace. And I did it. After that I spent many hours in front of that fireplace. It's Alaskan style, a very nice fireplace, but I prefer the one we had in that old house, because then, I looked ahead, and I had dreams; now I can only look back, and because I have such a bad memory, I don't even do that well.

But, what the hell, a man doesn't have to feel sad, Old Martin doesn't want to come to tears remembering the old days, because if he does, they'll tell him he's getting senile. Besides, from now on, it won't be the same, because now Old Martin remembers a lot of things. From now on, I'll feel cozier in front of that Alaskan-style fireplace. And speaking of that, that fire matter, Kathleen and I have come to agree completely. My son, though, is more of a television fan. Jimmy, half-and-half.

But anyway, winter was always sad in the old country. Our ears were always blue from the cold and our hands totally chapped. But I am sick of winter stories and I am going to move on to summer.

Summer used to be very cheerful, *oso alaia,* and even more cheerful around July, because that's when the town's festival would take place. Old Martin can't explain just how *alaiak* the festivals were, but that's all I wish for Jimmy, for him to be able to experience the same kind of excitement we felt every year for the festivities. Someone might say: "Old Martin, you were only loggers who hadn't been anywhere, and you went wild over anything. You thought that a few fireworks exploding in the sky were the biggest show on earth. And what was that after all? Nothing."

Old Martin would agree: "Yes, sir; *bai, jauna,* you are completely right, I really appreciate your opinion. We thought those were the best fireworks in the world because we didn't see fireworks very often reaching all the way to the sky, leaving a trail of smoke behind and whistling as they took off. Yes, sir; *bai, jauna.*"

Perhaps someone else would tell me: "Come on, Old Martin, how can you feel proud of those town holidays? Because you had coffee and pastries? We have them every day here and we don't brag about it."

Old Martin would gladly answer this one, too: "Yes, sir, you are also completely right, I really appreciate your opinion. It's true that we had coffee and pastries only at festival time. *Bai, jauna.*"

And if a third one came saying: "You were very backwards people, Old Martin, half savage, always eating broad beans. So, it isn't surprising you went crazy once a year when things changed a little bit."

"It isn't a bit surprising," Old Martin would answer, "*ez, jauna.*" Ours was a very hard life, and when we heard the big church bell toll, calling us to the celebrations, when we heard the tolling of that bell, which, by the way, was supposedly the biggest in the whole province, with that elegant chime, we would shiver from head to toe. We would have goose bumps, even me, and hold on! . . . *kontuz, jauna!* Old Martin is not a sentimental man at all. I am not like one of those dummies that get all misty-eyed over

anything; Old Martin is not like the winners on those
TV game shows. He's not stupid, but he would get
goose bumps, and the shivers all over his body. Old
Martin would like to face those three gentlemen and
ask them one question: "If it's not too much to ask,
gentlemen, what is Fort Knox?"

"Fort Knox? Why, that is the place where all the
gold in the country is kept."

"Do you gentlemen know what Old Martin likes
most of all? Do you know I love money?"

"Of course we do. The whole neighborhood
knows that."

"Well, listen to this. Old Martin wouldn't trade
the longing he felt for those festivals for all the gold
in Fort Knox. No way, *ez horixe!*" Then they would
understand what kind of feelings we had for those celebrations. I have to tell Kathleen: "Jimmy will have
more celebrations than me, he'll eat pastries every day,
he'll see more fireworks, but he'll never experience that
thrill I had." And that she would have to do her best as
an *ama* to give him things to look forward to.

That's what my wife used to say, too. Poor Maria,
Maria *gaixoa!* She was also very stubborn, same as my
daughter-in-law—women have always been hardheaded in my family, *emakumeak!* "Like pure stone,"
that's what I'd tell my son. They are good women,
bai horixe, but hardheaded. She always used to tell
me, "Martin"—that's how she called me, Old Martin and the other nicknames came later—"Martin,"
she used to say to me, "I would also like to have a
little excitement. Here I live without anything to look

forward to; without dreams, and dreams are three-quarters of life. You are taking away three-quarters of my life with your obsession about staying out here." Of course, she wanted to get off the ranch. She didn't like it there, no shops, no drugstores, no beauty parlors. She wanted to come here, to Boise, to have all those things. Maria was very curious.

"Come on, Maria! Doesn't the thought that we are saving a few bucks by living and working out here help you go on?"

"Not at all," that hardheaded woman would answer.

Maybe I'm greedy and stingy, always after money, the more the better. As I've said before, I didn't want to leave the mountains, my life was there. We finally came down to town, and what makes me saddest of all is that it was too late for my poor wife because two years after we came down here, she died, hit by a car. Maria *gaixoa*! But she loved being in Boise, getting to visit all the drugstores and beauty parlors, and that's the only thing that comforts me when I think of those days. Old Martin, I tell myself, It would've been worse if she had died the very day after you came. And, anyway, if we had come down to town earlier, who knows, that car could have hit her sooner. You never know how things are going to turn out. But I've gone too far with this talk of hopes and dreams, now it's time to talk about those years in the Basque Country, and the story about the fight between Iharra and Beltza.

As I was saying before, the *festak* broke our daily routine, and we used to do things out of character: I used to smoke, and Iharra used to dance. Everybody else did something different from their everyday life. We used to drink a lot too, shot after shot, *zurruta* as we say in Basque. Of course after so much *zurruta* we used to get a little drunk and naturally we would start looking for fights. We mostly fought people from out of town. If an outsider happened to be in town, Beltza or someone else would shout at him: "Eh, you son of a bitch! What are you coming to this town for? To steal our girls?"

Sometimes that would scare them off, but other times not. Then we would take turns fighting. For example, Beltza used to start the fight; if he happened to be defeated, which almost never happened, someone else would jump in, until the outsider gave up. Once he surrendered, we would throw him into the fountain; in the meantime, while we were busy at the fountain, the bar owner could clean up the bar. He cleaned the mess on the floor of his place the best he could. Sometimes, when there were four or five outsiders, the floor would end up full of broken glass—not because we threw the glasses on the floor, but because those were fair fights, let me tell you, not like the ones where those blacks pull a knife on you before you realize it. *Ez, jauna,* not us, we were fair. But of course, if glasses fall down they break, and that's just what happened there. Other times, if a fight broke out when people were smoking cigars, the floor ended up covered with brown tobacco leaves. But the bartender

would clean everything while we were finishing with the fountain business; it felt great to come back to the bar.

In the afternoon, the music would start up and in a while a little band would come in to play waltzes. It was OK to dance close in the *festak*. Girls used to pretend they were having a great time together by themselves, giggling and dancing one with another, totally ignoring the guys around them. But if we went and asked them for a dance, they'd be holding us tight before we even finished asking them the question. They were dying to dance with us, but of course they had to pretend they were not. Women, *emakumeak*!

That year, when Iharra and Beltza got mad at each other, the band didn't come until late. On top of that, no outsiders showed up, so no fights, no nothing. Then an old man appeared in town with a horse and a cart. The rumors began:

"Have you heard that he's bringing one of those stones used in lifting contests?"

"A rock or a steel cylinder?" we wondered, because until then, we were only familiar with those that lifted steel with the strength of their grip, and betting on that kind. We didn't know about the stone lifters.

That kind of competition in the Old Country consisted of lifting a stone or steel cylinder of a hundred kilos or more from the ground up to the shoulder as many times as possible in a set period. Everyone got excited, because people made big bets, betting money, land, cattle, some even everything they had. It was high stakes gambling.

All the young people headed for the old man who stood with his horse, to see the weight, and so did we three, Iharra, Beltza, and me. It was a good-looking, smooth, cylindrical stone. Underneath, it had two slots for your hands so you could lift it. Since people were a little bored that day, they asked the old man, who always organized those kinds of competitions and bets, if he could put the stone down on the ground, so people could try to lift it. Of course Beltza led the way.

"I bet you I can lift it four times in a minute!"

People surrounded him. Since Beltza was very arrogant, he took that bet very seriously; he took off his shirt, breathed a few times and grabbed the rock.

All he was thinking about at that moment was women, *emakumeak,* what else? He wanted very much to impress them. He lifted the stone up to his shoulder four times within the time he promised. Beltza took a few more deep breaths and put his shirt back on, smiling as if he had really accomplished something. And suddenly, out of the blue, Iharra said, "I want to try it, too."

Iharra wasn't that kind of a person, he wasn't a bettor, he wasn't a show-off at all. When he started removing his shirt we knew he was going to try it. He had no sooner gotten close to the stone, when Beltza walked over to it and, acting really surprised, started making fun of him.

"Come on, Iharra, what are you doing?"

"Don't you see, or what?" said Iharra, without taking his eyes off the stone.

And then Beltza roared, "You want to lift the rock? Get out of here, you're nothing but skin and bones."

"Just wait and see," answered Iharra humbly, but you could see he was beginning to get mad.

"Don't do it, Iharra. Don't even try," said Beltza, grabbing Iharra's arm in a mocking way as if he didn't want him to get close to the stone. Everybody was staring at them. The girls were giggling. "Don't start playing around, Iharra! You are going to hurt yourself! You are going to break yourself in half!"

I thought Beltza had gone too far teasing Iharra. One had only to look at Iharra's face to realize that. You could see anger in the eyes; if the eyes start moving back and forth, as if they can't find the right spot to stop, watch out! And Iharra's eyes were moving like that.

"Leave me alone!" Iharra said all of a sudden, pushing Beltza out of the way. Now, Beltza was the one whose eyes were moving here and there, although he didn't have any reason to be angry. He had started everything after all, but as I said before, Beltza had a very bad temper. I told myself: "Martin, Martin, keep your nose out of this. This is going to get out of hand." And it did. Iharra lifted the cylinder only three times, and, of course, Beltza didn't miss the chance to tease him. He started laughing at him, trying to sound funny, but it didn't come out that way. Beltza didn't forget the shove.

"Now you are going to get sick, Iharra! You barely lifted the cylinder three times and now you're going to get sick. You look as pale as a sheet."

"You think you're a hell of a guy, don't you?" answered Iharra. Beltza ignored him, and turned toward the silly young women who could only giggle. "Look at Iharra. What a show-off!"

Phew, that's all we need, I thought. I smelled trouble. At that point I didn't know things were going to turn out the way they did. It was obvious that those two friends of mine were going to get mad at each other. But nobody thought that they would end up in the plaza, facing each other in a fierce competition that would be the talk of the town. There was no one to blame but the old man who brought the stone to town.

There we were, Iharra and me. I was holding Iharra's sweater and trying to calm things down while he was putting his shirt on. I scolded him and told him that the both of them had acted like children and that I didn't expect such behavior. We could hear Beltza and his harem laughing.

"Beltza is a big-mouth, and he makes me sick!" said Iharra. He was really hurt. And as we talked, the old man who had brought the stone came up to us and asked if he might speak with us. "If it's all right, may I say a few words?" he began. The man sounded sincere, so both of us nodded yes.

"This time, that guy," pointing at Beltza, "made you look like a fool. But if you want to, he'll be the one who ends up looking like a fool, and not here

either, but in a big plaza, in front of thousands of people."

"He's up to something," I thought. Right away I smelled gambling in the old man's words.

"Could you get to the point, sir?" asked Iharra.

"You are better than he is, that's what it's all about. Today you've lifted one time less than he did, but in how much time? In one minute. Shit! *Kaka zaharra!* Let's see what would happen in half an hour. You're fit, nothing but muscle, you've got good wind. You'll beat that fat guy easy."

"Whew," I said to myself, "he's not joking." Looking at Beltza, no one would think he was fat at all. He was stout, but not fat. The old man said that for a reason, though. He wanted to draw Iharra into the wager. And that's exactly what happened.

"Are you talking about a bet?" Iharra looked very serious.

"Yes, if you want to make one. Look here, I am a member of a club. We would take you on and prepare you. We'll even put up the money. And you'll win the bet, no question about that. That will put a little change in your pocket. And besides, you'll make that big shot look like a fool."

The old man was speaking very slowly and softly.

"But, *jauna,* don't you know those two are friends? How can you make them start betting against each other?"

Neither of them paid any attention. By then, they were partners, without saying a word, they were already partners. "I'd better be careful," I thought, "if you stay here, Martin, you'll look as if you were on Iharra's side and against Beltza." And Old Martin doesn't like that, he didn't like it then, he doesn't like it now. When my son and Kathleen get mad and start yelling at each other, I always step aside, neither on one side, nor the other. That's the way I am. Some people may think that's no way to act, but it works for me.

"*Baietz,* I'll do it," said Iharra, and the old man extended his hand. When he tried to shake mine, I refused.

"Listen to me, old man," I said, "Iharra is my friend but Beltza is also my friend. I'd rather stay out of it."

"You're a coward," the old man said to me. He seemed to be a slick talker, and I am sure he was. But like a lot of slick talkers, he had a sharp tongue, the tongue of a snake.

"If you are friends with Beltza, tell him to come over here," he asked me promptly, and I did as he asked, because at that point it suited me. I wanted Beltza to see I was with both of them. He was talking loudly to the group of girls. I stopped a few meters from them and motioned for him to come over.

"Hey, you, come up here! Are you trying to give me orders, too?" He shouted at me. "Phew," I thought, "this one here is on fire, too." I went up to him and explained everything.

"Here we go!" said Beltza, pretending he was having fun. "So, Iharra wants to make a bet. I'm going to accept it. You don't get many chances to make money this easy."

I completely agreed with him on that; it's true, money doesn't grow on trees. There I was, dying to go to America, but without enough money to buy a ticket.

There's a fountain with four spouts near the plaza of Obaba and we gathered right there, my two friends, the old man, two more witnesses, and me. The girls also came after us because they smelled something cooking. The sound of the fountain hushed our words and gave our dealings a sense of secrecy. Those girls standing there were listening carefully to what we said.

"You know how things are," said the old man. Iharra was distracted, looking at one of the spouts as if something would come out any time. Beltza, on the other hand, was staring at the old man, nose to nose.

"Come on, old man, how much are we going to bet?"

"Twenty silver *duros*," he replied.

I started sweating. In those days, twenty silver *duros* was a lot of money, like a thousand dollars today. How many trips could I take on the boat to America with that money? I didn't need much time to figure that out, at least five trips. I jumped into the conversation.

"Wait a second, Beltza. And this goes for you, too, Iharra, so do me a favor and look over here." That's how I began and since I've always liked to talk, I was ready to start my speech, *bai, jauna.* "Remember

you've always been best friends up to now, think of how childish this is." I was prepared to keep on saying the same sort of things when the old man cut me off.

"Listen to him, sure, let's see what foolishness he comes up with."

Everybody laughed, even Iharra laughed a little bit, which was not very common for him. I felt left out.

"But it's just not right for two friends to bet against each other," I proposed.

Then Iharra countered, shouting: "And is it all right to make fun of friends? Are you saying that I should give in to his arrogance?"

Beltza couldn't keep quiet after hearing that. How could he?

"And who the hell are you?! Eh? What are you? A chicken shit! That's what you are, a chicken shit!"

He grabbed Iharra by the neck. That old man who seemed to be so smooth caught fire and shouted, warning Beltza to watch out for his hands because Iharra was now a member of their club and they didn't joke about those things. "No one is going to harm one of our members." He continued: "It's not a good idea to beat him up now. Wait for the contest in the plaza, see if you're man enough then."

"I'll take him on here and in the plaza, too. I would take care of you, too, if you weren't such an old goat. And don't you dare threaten me with that brotherhood business of yours, or else you'll shed some blood right here."

Beltza was terribly brave, no one could back him down. He had the same nature as a fox terrier Jimmy

had once; the more you tried to scare him away, the harder he tried to attack you. He didn't know how to back off.

That's how the challenge was made, and Beltza strutted away from the plaza with a girl tucked under each arm, as if he had just heard the best news of his life. I remained behind, staring at the horse that had pulled the cart. There he was, next to the fountain, grazing peacefully on thick grass. "There you go, Martin," I thought to myself, "he's the only one here that kept his head on his shoulders. You better follow his example."

In the days that followed, the townsfolk talked of nothing else. The news of my two friends spread quickly. And in less time than it took to say the words out loud, there were two groups formed in town. The ones who thought Beltza was better, or had sympathy for him, gathered around him, and the same thing happened among those who favored Iharra. There they went, up and down the streets, each sheepherder with his own flock. When they crossed paths, which was unavoidable because the town had only one street in those days, they didn't greet one another, pretending they were mad or didn't know each other. That's the kind of thing that betting brings with it. By evening things started looking really ugly, because of the drinking, *zurruta,* of course, everybody was filled to the point that the bartender had to threaten people, saying he was going to call the *mikeleteak,* the town cops. He said he never had seen such a big fight in his entire life. And the poor guy had seen a few.

I didn't join either of the two groups. "Martin, Martin," I told myself, "you're better off not sticking your nose into this at all." Betting is a nasty thing. That's what I thought then and that's what I still think now; I made it very clear to Kathleen once when the whole family went to Reno: the casino business is a very wasteful thing and unless you're foolish, you wouldn't put that much money in those *makinak*. Of course she had an answer waiting for me.

"And if you weren't so tight-fisted, we would live more peacefully at home."

"Don't you two start up with your discussions again. We came here to have fun!" my son interrupted us. Of course, he's also a big spender, just like his mother, *ama bezelakoxea*. She was a spendthrift, that was my Maria's only fault, poor Maria, Maria *gaixoa*.

"Do you have to throw your money away to have fun?" I asked him, and then I got angry. I also told him that I couldn't last one more second in that casino, that I was going to faint if we stayed there. I was out of control by then. After that, Kathleen took me to a pastry shop. She told me to stay there until they came back, and that I could eat all the chocolate puddings I wanted, so they could have some peace. There they left me, like an old dog in his house. I had five puddings, in revenge, because I was really mad at them. And then, of course, I got diarrhea and I had to stay in bed for five days.

"If I die, you'll have to explain it to God at the last judgment, because it will be your fault, *zure errua,* Kathleen. You'll have to come up with a great explanation."

But that's all over. It's better to forget about it and get back to my other story. I still think that what happened that day was strange. Until that stone showed up, all of us in town had lived in peace and harmony, always greeting one another warmly as if we were good friends: *Kaixo! Bizi al gara? Zer moduz? Epa!* But from the time we saw that stone and witnessed Beltza and Iharra's argument, you would have thought one half of the town had been the bitter enemy of the other for ages. That's what happens to people in primitive towns like that one. It was like there was a pocket of pus festering just under the skin, and when it suddenly burst, everything was smeared—respect, love, friendship, everything.

As I said before, I didn't like any of that, and kept to myself, dancing and so on. Besides, I'd become very popular among the young women because all the men were so wrapped up with the betting business that they ended up ignoring them. I felt sorry for Iharra because, from the beginning, Beltza's group was bigger. Beltza was more robust and braver so everybody joined up with him thinking he would be the winner. I am sure that if I had supported Iharra he would have been thankful for it, but I didn't want to take sides, *ez horixe* and when Old Martin says "no way" he means it. *Ez horixe!*

Beltza began training for the big competition at his own home and the man he chose to be his coach went with him. Iharra, on the other hand, moved to

the next town, to the home of the malicious old man. Both my friends quit working in the woods, and started training for hours on end, lifting stones.

I used to go visit them, first Iharra, then Beltza, talking to each of them by turn as they took breaks from their training routine. The competition made them both behave in a very serious way, as if they suddenly had grown up. Especially Beltza, he stopped cussing and threatening, his arrogant behavior disappeared. He never asked me about Iharra. And Iharra played the same game with Beltza. Since they were both young, the skin on their shoulders had not been toughened and both of them suffered a lot of pain from the stones. During the first forty-some days when I visited with them, I would notice traces of blood on the shoulder areas of their white shirts.

I had a great time at the beginning. Both of them let me watch them training. It was very entertaining and I really enjoyed it. First, I would go to work in the woods, then have a bite to eat, and toward the evening, since the weather was great in the summer, I would go for a walk to watch my friends training. There was always something new. I always went back home with a different story to tell. To mention one, Iharra used to jump rope, but not with a rope like little girls, but with a stick.

"Is that true?" asked my mother, amazed. "He must have a very strong back."

"And Beltza," I continued, "he hangs from a tree branch and he does chin-ups, kissing the branch a hundred times."

My mother would tell stories about my father, who used to be very strong in his day. I was having a great time going from one to another, on good terms with one and on good terms with the other. I knew all their secrets. Only a few people were allowed near the training ground, and not many knew exactly how things were going. All they heard were rumors: Beltza had lifted so many times, Iharra had made terrific improvement, and so on. Most of the time I was the source.

But all that ended after the first month. As soon as the first stage of the training was completed, each coach approached me, first the mean old man and then, a little later, Beltza's.

"You coward," the old man shouted, "you're having a good time, aren't you?"

I answered, feigning innocence: "Not too bad, no."

"That's good; do you see that little road there?"

He pointed toward the path that led from his house down the hill to town.

By then it was early fall, and the ferns had begun to turn red.

"The one that crosses the woods?" I asked, faking a very innocent look.

"That very one—lovely trail, eh?"

"I wouldn't call it an ugly one."

When it doesn't suit Old Martin to understand something, he can have a hard time. For instance, when Kathleen says:

"There's a bunch of mice in this house! Haven't you noticed?"

Every time she says something like that I play the innocent one, looking out the window, as if I saw a little bird in my mimosa. And she keeps going:

"What amazes me is that those mice are able to open the fridge! I didn't know there was such a mouse."

I keep staring at the imaginary little bird on the mimosa branch, as if I were thinking, "*Txori polita*, what a beautiful bird!"

"That's nothing for Mickey Mouse," says poor Jimmy. Then Kathleen continues: "The most amazing thing is the taste those mice have. Even though there are many different kinds of cheese in the fridge, they always pick something else, a piece of apple pie, chocolate pudding, a piece of cake."

Finally, when Kathleen says that, Old Martin, still staring at the mimosa branch as if it were no big deal, says: "It wasn't a mouse, Kathleen, it was me."

"Oh, really? Thank God, I was starting to get frightened! I thought all the animals had rebelled."

"That's true," poor Jimmy informs us, "the animals have rebelled." A mother is a mother. And Kathleen is a mother, Jimmy's.

"Why do you say that, Jimmy?"

"Because yesterday in school . . ."

And the kid starts telling one of his stories. They are always very strange, I don't know what kind of friends and teachers he has but that's another issue. I wanted to say that my strategy is to let time take

care of things, I know after a while something always comes up. If every time Kathleen wants to scold me, she ends up worrying about the boy, it will become harder for her to get after me. She will think twice before she picks on me, maybe three times.

When I was young I used to follow the same strategy. I used to pretend I was stupid and wait for something to come up. That old man wanted to get me out of there, he didn't like having me there checking on the marks his pupil was making, but because he wasn't making himself clear, I just kept pretending I didn't know what was going on.

Of course, my tactic doesn't always work. And that day, I had to take off down that path through the ferns at once, because the old man told me, screwing up his face, "Follow that path and get the hell home. We don't need you nosing around here."

A few days later, Beltza's coach gave me the same order: "This is none of your business! Get lost!"

But it had already become a habit for me. I couldn't quit, I had to see how my friends were improving. I started to spy on them by turn. First, I spied on Iharra; next, on Beltza. I went to the sessions every day. I would lie down somewhere close to where they were training, look up at the stars, sharpen my ears, and keep track of the progress my friends made.

Since at that time I didn't own a watch, I timed them with my heartbeat. I had gone to the doctor and asked him:

"I would like to know how many times my heart beats in a minute, *jauna*."

The man was a little surprised, but he was a quiet man and he didn't feel the need to ask me anything. He timed my heart, wrote a number down on a piece of paper and handed it to me. Forty-five beats.

Once I found that out, toward evening, I hid myself in the woods, close to the house, listening carefully. At first I would listen to every single noise in the woods. It seemed like everything was quiet but after a while, when I paid attention, I could make out all sorts of noises. Then, a little bit later, all the noises went away except the one I was interested in, the one made by the stone being thrown back to the padding on the ground: dop! . . . dop! . . . dop! . . . That was all I could hear. The stone from the ground to the shoulder, and from the shoulder to the ground, dop! Up, down, and then, dop! Once more, the heavy stone carried right up to the shoulder and, dop! . . .

Then I would put one of my hands on the other wrist and start counting. At first it was very hard to do, but after a few days I got accustomed to it and after two weeks I had it down. Thanks to this system I realized that Iharra lifted the stone nineteen or twenty times in five minutes; Beltza, though, could lift it twenty-four times and even more. Resting among the ferns, looking at the stars, I felt sorry for Iharra, and thought to myself, people were right from the beginning when, during the *festak,* Beltza attracted more people to his side. Beltza was going to beat him. At least, if Iharra didn't improve in the remaining days before the competition. But I kept quiet. When I went to the bar, I would take a look at the bets writ-

ten down on the blackboard hanging on the wall; all
of them favored Beltza. The only remaining question
was how many more lifts Beltza would make than
Iharra. Everybody thought they knew who the winner would be. I felt very sorry for Iharra because all
that hard work, sweating and bleeding, was going to
be useless.

I don't remember how many days it was before
the contest, maybe twenty or so, when the old man
became suspicious of me. Perhaps he heard me moving about by the house, perhaps he saw my tracks,
the trampled ferns or footprints on the muddy path.
I don't know, the thing is that somehow he figured
out that I had been snooping around.

As soon as he realized that, he had a young boy
from his club make a few false blows.

If I ever tell this story to my family and I get to
this point, Jimmy will ask, "What is a false blow,
aitite?" And I am sure my son and Kathleen will wonder too.

"Pass me a little pudding," I'll ask then, know-
ing that not even that hardheaded Irish woman will
disappoint me in the middle of such an interesting
story. I'll eat the pudding, and then I'll get back to
explaining the false blow.

"One guy lifts the stone for real while another
one makes a sound like a lift, that's the false blow."
The old man was suspicious that someone might spy
on the training and he didn't want anyone to know
who was doing better, which of course was what I
was doing. That's why he had that other guy lift-

ing another stone at the same time as Iharra. Two guys, two stones, two blows, and whoever tried to listen didn't know which blow was which, and it was impossible to guess.

From then on I didn't hear the single, regular, dop . . . dop . . . dop . . . but a series of them, dop . . . dop, dop, dop . . . dop, dop . . ., and I lost track of Iharra's progress.

But anyway, I didn't quit my spying. Now I did it just for the heck of it. Sure, I knew I wouldn't be able to find out anything about the competition; I guess I was used to spending half the night surrounded by ferns, lying there, under the stars, smelling the scent the woods give off toward dark, and dreaming about my trip to this country, about the boat that some day I was going to take. I remember once a leaf woke me when it brushed my face. It was autumn, after all. I guess that time I had even fallen asleep—just think how far my fantasies had taken me!

Besides all that, it was a wonderful thing to be there in the woods listening to the sound of those two stones, there in the emptiness of the night; the beat of the stones along with my own heartbeat, all those beats becoming one.

In the meantime, the day of the competition was getting closer. You could tell by all the commotion in town. It didn't seem to be the same isolated town as before. Outsiders showed up, attracted by the betting, by the smell of easy money. A week or so before the contest, almost everybody was betting that Beltza would lift the stone five times more than Iharra; some

people even bet that he would lift it ten times more. But no one knew anything for sure, not even me. The old man's trick had kept me from following Iharra's progress.

And then what had to happen did happen. I don't know how I didn't see it coming before, being as sharp as I was, but I guess I didn't suspect anything. I'm going to explain it, but no one should think Old Martin is stupid, and if, when I tell Kathleen the story, she starts making fun of me, and if anyone else does it, I'll tell them, "If your Irish father had happened to be there, and he had dared to take part in the betting, he would even have lost his balls."

"Please!" she'll tell me, "That's offensive!"

She'll stand up, leave the table and go to her room, for she has done it for less reason than that. Later, she'll make me go for a week with no pudding. But I can't help it. I can't stand her father, I just can't. Besides no one likes to be taken for a fool.

Well, the thing was that the bet was fixed from the beginning. If I had thought more about how the old man acted, if I would have looked more closely at those snake eyes, I would have suspected something. But all I thought about were my two friends.

Yes, that old man had everything fixed from the very beginning. When he first saw Beltza and Iharra challenge each other during the same festival, I am sure he thought, "Look at those two naive young men, and that Iharra looks so hurt. Here you have a great opportunity for the old-time gamblers!" Of course. We didn't have many coaches in that isolated town, and he, the old fox, knew all of them for sure. It wouldn't take much for him to control the whole situation.

I discovered it by chance. Because I was lucky. When I was lying down in the woods next to Beltza's house, surrounded by ferns, thinking about my trip to America, I sensed someone coming up the road, breathing. I mean, breathing heavily like someone climbing a hill. Even though there wasn't a full moon, it was almost full, and by its light I recognized the person walking. I was astonished. It was the devilish old man. Why was he, Iharra's coach, coming to Beltza's house? I asked myself, and at that very same moment, I figured out what I hadn't seen clearly until then; the bet was fixed.

The old man walked very slowly toward the door of the house; he stopped there for a few seconds, to catch his breath, I guess. Then he knocked on the door. Beltza's coach opened the door. Without exchanging a word, the two of them started walking down the road, in silence. When they had walked ten steps down the road, they stopped, right close to me. I was lucky, as I said before.

Only the old man spoke. It was very clear he was in charge.

"How is Beltza doing?"

"He's been lifting the stone sixty-five times in three periods, twenty-five in the first one, then twenty-two, and eighteen in the last one. In the last period he really falls off, he's left completely spent."

"On the other hand, Iharra doesn't wear out, he's been lifting the stone almost the same number of times in each of the three periods, twenty-three, twenty-two, and in the last one twenty-one or twenty-two."

"Almost like Beltza."

"I didn't expect everything to work out so well. Good, good, everything looks great."

And the old man let out a laugh, a very disgusting laugh. Of course things looked great for them. They, the people from both clubs, would bet on Iharra, because the money, lots of money was wagered on Beltza. It was perfect for them that Beltza wore down in the last period. In the first turn he would be way ahead, people would bet even more on him, and in the last one he would be completely worn out, even more than in training because, of course, that was what they were there for.

"Did you talk to that girl?" asked the old man, and he mentioned the name of that hot-blooded girl Beltza used to walk home with.

"She's there right now," and he pointed to the house.

The old man laughed again, as disgusting as before. "It's obvious that kind of stuff takes a lot out of a man." Then he mentioned the pre-contest meal. The other guy said he would feed him very heavy food. Before they left, the old man brought up the matter of the waist support. They were talking about one of the rituals that takes place before every weight-lifting session, when the trainer of the lifter wraps his

waist tightly with a wide sash to give support to the stomach and back.

"In the first period," said the old man, "fasten his sash higher than it should be, just a little higher, five centimeters will be enough. You have to make him break down, even if he lifts twenty-seven times, wear him down. If you tie his sash the way I tell you, he'll be exhausted. He'll break down in the second period."

"That's a deal."

"Deal."

And with that, they said goodbye, without even shaking hands. The old man went back down the hill and started whistling a little song. Naturally, he was happy.

I, on the other hand, was terrified. I felt like standing up from the bushes and yelling out loud, shouting out to make Beltza come to the window, so I could tell him, "Beltza, Beltza, they set you up, the bet is fixed, and you are going to be the loser, back out of it, and make peace with Iharra."

"Is that true?" Beltza would have said, astonished.

"Yes, man, it's true."

"Then I'm going to kill both of them, first my coach and then the old man! I'm going to kill them right now! Wait a minute, I'm going to get my axe!"

I am sure he would have had that kind of reaction, if I had told him, but, of course, I didn't.

Old Martin, as I said from the beginning, Old Martin has always had his own way of thinking, throughout his whole life, that's how Old Martin is.

You say some people like to do things without thinking? That's OK with me, that's their own business.
I say the same thing to Kathleen: you can do whatever you feel like doing, I don't care, go ahead, Kathleen! If one of those black beggars comes knocking
on your door, and you give him a dollar, so be it, it's
OK, but then if he spends the dollar getting drunk,
heads home and beats up his wife, and then his five
or six kids (those black beggars have a bunch of kids),
then, as I said, his five or six children start crying and
yelling, then, you think about it, Kathleen: it's your
fault, because you and your dollar are responsible for
bringing such grief to that black man's house.

I was the same way when I was young. I used to
think carefully about everything beforehand, I didn't
want to cause trouble when trying to do some good.

Martin, Martin, I told myself, what's going to
happen if you tell Beltza about the scam and he starts
swinging the axe? Well, then something really serious
will happen, someone will get killed. Then, they'll
take Beltza to jail, that's if they don't hang him, and
if they don't hang him he'll rot in jail for sure, and
then what? Martin, what a great favor you did him!
And even if he doesn't kill anyone, won't it still be a
terrible mess? Because the old man and the other guy
would deny everything—"We don't know where you
got that vicious rumor. The issue here is that Beltza
is scared to death and that he wants to back out. So,
back out if you want to, but first pay the room and
board for these last three months and all the other
expenses."

What could I do then? Nothing, I would have to take money from my own pocket and feel ashamed in front of the whole town. What would the gamblers say then? Who knows what they would say, they would be so mad because the bets would be off. It would be a very bad situation for everybody, most of all for me, because people would say, "Do you know who's been stirring everything up? Do you know who started this story about the bet being fixed? That Martin guy, the one who always dreams about going to America."

"Oh, really?" the others would say. "We'd better give him a little present before he leaves. Next Sunday, after the dance, we should beat the hell out of him!"

That might happen to you, Martin, and that's where your good intentions will end up causing a complete disaster. Martin, you're too honest, you're too good-hearted, and it hurts to see both of your friends in such a situation, one against the other and, worst of all, cheated, but things have gone too far and now it's too late to turn back. Besides, didn't Iharra and Beltza decide on their own about the bet? Did they listen to you when you told them not to go ahead with all that? Not one bit. Then it's better to keep what you know to yourself and head home.

That was the conclusion of all my pondering, and what I thought of doing, I did. I went home and got into bed. My conscience was clear.

As I have said more than once during that time, I was blessed with good luck, and that is the truest thing I've written on this paper. That night I dreamed of my trip to America and the money I was going to make there. I slept great. When I woke up next morning, though, I felt sad, *zoritxarrekoa*.

Martin, Martin, dreams are beautiful, but a waste of time. You'll never get the money for the passage, that's an expensive trip.

I had no sooner said this to myself, when I remembered the bet.

"But, Martin, why didn't you think of it before! The bet is your only hope! Scrape up all the money in your house and bet it on Iharra."

I jumped out of my bed. Twenty-four hours later I had made lots of bets, with both local people and outsiders. I picked the richest ones of all, because you might not get paid if you bet with poor people.

The day of the contest finally came, and just as absolutely everybody had expected, there were more people in town than ever before. The plaza was closed off and more than three thousand people had their eyes fixed on the stone. I went to one of the back rows, a little apart from everybody else. I didn't want to be able to see Iharra and Beltza face to face. It would have made me too sad. Nevertheless, I saw them entering the plaza; they looked as white as ghosts and very serious, each of them with his towel, a wide sash for support, and a padded vest for protection. I also saw the old man and greeted him. "See you later, old man!" He seemed astonished seeing the smile on my lips. He acted like he wanted to ask me something, but he would have had to pass through a lot of people in order to approach me, so he didn't try. People were

screaming and shouting all over the place. I think that old man was very smart and he understood what my smile meant.

Old man, you can fool all these jackasses, but you won't fool me, no way, *ez horixe!*

In the first period, Beltza lifted the stone twenty-seven times, and Iharra only twenty-three. But in the second one, while Iharra again made twenty-three lifts, Beltza only lifted it seventeen times. There was a tremendous silence in the plaza. Almost everyone had bet on Beltza, and he was behind.

In the third and last period, the crowd really encouraged Beltza. They cheered him, the whole plaza bending and leaning back with him as he crouched under the stone and leaned back to lift it off the ground. But he only managed fifteen, and Iharra twenty.

When the competition was over, as strong as Beltza was, he started crying, right there, in front of everybody. Even some of the people in the plaza were crying. I even felt like crying, but I didn't let myself. To tell the truth, I had every reason to feel happy. I had enough money, more than enough, to buy my passage.

Three months later, I embarked for America. But before I left, I said goodbye to Iharra and Beltza. "It really makes me sad," I said to each of them, "to see that I'm leaving and you two are still mad at each other."

"There's nothing you can do about it," they both told me.

They were resigned to it. And that's what happened, they remained mad at each other for the rest of their lives. I was tempted to write them a letter from here, but since I always thought I was going to go back, I didn't think it was the right thing to do.

That's the only thing Old Martin didn't figure out quite right, not thinking that he might decide to stay here, in America, for the rest of his life, *betirako*. If I had decided to stay from the beginning, I would have written that letter to my friends, I would have done so many things differently, like learn English for example, *bai jauna*.

If I knew English well, I could tell Jimmy, in marvelous words, this whole story that I've put down on paper. But with my English, I'm not sure, maybe I won't tell him anything; besides, I am sure Kathleen would scold me because of the way I acted, she would treat me like a selfish old man. Because Kathleen doesn't know anything about the ups and downs of life.

BERNARDO ATXAGA

When a Snake
Stares at a Bird

When a snake stares at a bird, the bird is blinded, and the small world he had within his vision—a few trees, two or three roofs, the road, the blue of the sky—is suddenly hidden from him. The same as happens with the side-show magician's handkerchiefs: one minute everything is there—colors, movement, light—the next, everything is gone, nothing but emptiness remains.

The bird thinks that night has come upon him and that the evil glowing that blinds him is a star in the middle of that night. He is not aware of the snake, nor the hypnotic spell it casts. He prefers to believe in a simple lie, perhaps because the truth would be too hard.

Blinded, the bird begins to dance. But his movement bears no resemblance to that of a dancer. He looks like a drunk lost among the leaves, flapping his wings loudly, bumping them against the branches. He twists his neck until it nearly cracks, and sings clumsily, unable to carry a tune.

The snake and the bird, both are blameless. They are driven by a law that is older than the ocean and the mountains, there is nothing they can do but obey it. The law commands the snake to hunt gold finches, wrens, and robins and, with equal determination, to hide from the claws of the sparrow hawk. In the same way, the law directs the bird to worms as food, and to snakes as enemies. The law is the same for all creatures that draw breath in the world.

So, when a snake stares at a bird, it is merely an episode in an eternal fight. Farmers or solitary hikers who wander along the trails often see scenes of such a fight and think nothing of them. They look once and continue about their business . . .

Sebastian, however, was not a farmer and, at fourteen, was not in the habit of hiking on the trails. He had spent his entire life in the city and had been in the hills of Obaba for only three days. When he looked at the orchard and noticed the bird crazily bouncing among the apple blossoms, his heart jumped. He was amazed.

"What's wrong with that bird, Grandpa Martin?"

The grandfather was old, too old, at least, to walk under his own power, so his answer came from atop a donkey named Fangio that used to carry him around.

"Hurry. Throw a rock at him!"

Sebastian did not follow his grandfather's command right away. He felt for that clumsy bird the natural love that young people feel for animals, and he held the rock in his hand, not being able to bring himself to throw it. He did not have a lot of faith in Grandfather Martin, having met him only three days before, when he arrived in Obaba. As his father used to say, his mind was mixed up.

"The blood doesn't reach his brain very well," his father would say after every dinner when the conver-

sation turned toward the ups and downs of his mother's family from Obaba. His mother would defend the grandfather and his father would always make the same argument.

"Your father's mind is not working right, woman! How else do you explain his obsession with going to Terranova?"

"We all have our dreams," sighed his mother.

"But not that crazy!" his father would say, becoming angry. "To go to Terranova, and at his age!"

That was the kind of information Sebastian had about his grandfather Martin. That was why, in fact, he hesitated when he was asked to throw the rock. Sebastian was starting to feel tired. Since arriving in town he had done nothing but follow his grandfather's donkey all over. He already missed the way of life he left behind in the city, especially sleeping late on vacation since his aunt in Obaba would make him get up at nine every day.

Judging by the sun, he calculated that it must have been six o'clock in the evening. Where would he have been if he had stayed in the city for vacation? Perhaps at the movies, perhaps at home lying on the couch.

"Throw the rock!"

The grandfather was very skinny, and an even skinnier neck connected his head to his body. That neck, whitened by a badly shaved beard, was very tense when Sebastian heard the scream and became frightened.

Sebastian took three steps ahead, and his grand-father stood up over Fangio's ears. When the rock, after making its arc, hit a leaf above the bird, the grandfather began clapping.

"Get out, bird! Get out of there right away!"

"I didn't hit him," said Sebastian.

"Hit him? Who said you had to hit him? Look at the bird!"

From the top of a walnut tree, the robin looked far out into the world. There they were once again, right there, the roofs, the blue of the sky, right there, the road, Sebastian, the grandfather, and Fangio. The night that had fallen so suddenly and that shiny star in the middle of the night, seemed gone forever.

"The snake had bewitched him!"

"The snake?" asked Sebastian.

"Sure, the snake! When a snake stares at a bird, the bird becomes mesmerized!"

Sebastian was going to ask about him saving the bird by throwing the rock, but his grandfather began talking.

"When your rock hit the leaves and made a noise, you disturbed the snake, and it took its eyes off the robin. That's how you saved him."

Sebastian had more questions in mind to ask. What if the rock would have hit the bird? How did Grandpa know he was going to miss? But his grandfather was already on to other things: he was whistling.

"Here comes the robin!"

After heading toward the sky, the bird changed his direction, flying toward the earth in smaller and smaller circles. He finally landed on Grandfather Martin's shoulder.

For almost fifteen minutes, Sebastian witnessed this scene: his grandfather made half-spoken, half-whistling sounds to the robin, who answered back, singing in the grandfather's ear. They looked as if they were two old friends telling each other stories.

"Get out of here you crazy thing! Get out of here!" said the grandfather with the tone of those defending themselves from a compliment. The bird jumped to Fangio's head, and then took off. Little by little, his form disappeared into the blue of the sky. The grandfather, forehead wrinkled in a frown, watched Sebastian.

"And you, what are you doing here?"

Sebastian was not in his familiar streets, nor with his everyday friends. He was in an unknown village, with a grandfather he just met. His voice cracked when he answered.

"I came with you."

"Really? Who are you?"

"Me?"

"Yes, you!"

The grandfather watched him with a very serious expression, mounted atop Fangio.

"I'm . . . I'm your grandson. My aunt told you to show me the town, and that's why I'm here."

The grandfather stopped, as if deep in thought, and Sebastian remembered his father's suspicion: that blood didn't fully reach his brain.

"Oh, sure!" and a smile came to his lips. "You are the grandson that came to spend his vacation!"

"That's right!"

"Good! Good! Pardon me, Sebastian, sometimes things slip my mind!" and he continued, sighing, "There's nothing worse than getting older."

"It's OK, Grandpa Martin. What are we going to do next?"

"You want to go home, don't you?"

Sebastian had already forgotten about being tired and bored, all he wanted now was to know one thing, to find out what happened in that last episode with the robin.

"What were you doing with the robin? Talking with him?"

"A robin? What robin . . . ? Oh, sure, the robin!"

The grandfather looked at the tree where the bird had been dancing and his face brightened as if he remembered something.

"We'll go home soon, Grandson, but first I have something to do. Wait for me right here!" He kicked his donkey and entered the orchard. After a little while, he was shouting in a way that made the veins in his neck tremble. Sebastian could only make out a few sentences here and there.

"You're full of nothing but desires and vices. You're just a petty thief!"

The grandfather was really upset and, menac-
ingly, he shook the stick normally reserved for Fangio.
Although Sebastian watched the orchard carefully,
just as before, he did not see anything but the ground
carpeted by apples. At whom was his grandfather
shouting? At the snake that wanted to eat the robin?
Worried, he approached his grandfather. And then,
right then, he saw the snake, erect, its head bowed. It
looked like a greenish stick planted in the ground.

"Sorry? Sure you're sorry! Excuses! You're a glutton! That's all!" The questions piled up. Hadn't his
grandfather talked with the robin? And the snake,
wasn't he humbly accepting the scolding? What kind
of a bond did his grandfather have with animals?
Then, for the second time, he found himself fixed in
his grandfather's sharp gaze.

"And you? What are you doing here?"

Sebastian improvised a theory about what was
happening: every time his grandfather talked to the
animals, he forgot people, locals as well as foreigners.
And when he talked to people, the animals would slip
from his mind.

"Do I have to repeat it, Grandpa Martin? I'm
Sebastian, your grandson."

"You don't say?" The grandfather was totally
astonished.

"Of course I am."

Little by little he started to come to his senses.

"The one from the city?"

"Yes, Grandpa, yes!"

"Good! Good! And you told me you're sorry, is that right?"

"Sorry?"

Sebastian wanted to say no, that the one feeling sorry was the snake and not him, but he thought it would be smarter to keep such a strange thought to himself.

"Let's go back to town!" The grandfather sounded cheerful. "If you're upset, you've got to go to the tavern!"

It was seven in the evening. Even though the sun still dominated the largest part of the earth, the shadows had already begun what would be, with the nightfall a few hours later, a total conquest. The river was dark, and dark likewise were the mountain ridges covered with pines. By then, the sky in the east had already lost its lively early morning color and a timid blue followed the green of the hills.

People were working in the fields without paying attention to the threat of the shadow. Some women removed weeds from the alfalfa fields. Further away, where fields extended across the countryside, harvesters bowed toward the earth, creator and master of us all. Dogs and swallows were engaged in competition, barks following shrieks. The smell of the newly born fern spread from the woods to the air.

From the height of his seat astride Fangio, the grandfather whispered a psalm-like melody, and Sebastian pretended to look for wild strawberries. He only pretended because strawberries are hidden fruits, and it was impossible for him to give the attention that such a task required. His thoughts were else-where, with his grandfather's conversations, first with the bird, and then with the snake.

On top of that, Sebastian realized something else as he walked to town. As they passed in front of the houses, chained dogs stopped barking and, as if they were seeing someone they knew, wagged their tails. So, thought Sebastian, all the dogs in Obaba know Grandpa Martin.

But for the time being he remained quiet. He preferred to keep pretending to look for strawberries.

All the lights of the tavern were on by the time they arrived in the plaza of Obaba. Sebastian had a dark thought as he helped his grandfather get off the donkey: how could a man that weighed so little still be alive? That shriveled body seemed to be made out of paper. But as the grandfather said, "So, you're upset," he laughed calmly, and that calm took over before the dark thought had enough time to ripen.

"Let's go, Grandson! Let's forget our sadness!"

There were ten men lined up at the bar and four more playing cards at what seemed to be a marble table. Some looked at the grandfather. Others, most of them, looked at Sebastian. The young man who had just arrived from the city sensed something like envy or admiration in the looks of those quiet men who hardly knew the world, and he felt important. That feeling, so intense, penetrated to the very core of his heart, and he made his way to the bar as if he had rehearsed it before.

"Get him some wine!" ordered the grandfather.

"Wine?" asked the woman behind the bar.

"To take the sadness away, woman, to take the sadness away!" said the grandfather.

"Sadness? What could a young man like him be sad about?"

"Just get the wine!" interrupted Sebastian.

Somehow, he felt mysterious, or at least he wished he were. After all, he felt the temptation anyone feels when they are in an unknown place: he wanted to try on a new personality. This was his first time inside a bar. He drank his first, half-filled glass in one swallow.

"Very good, Grandson! Leave the whole bottle here, woman!"

"The whole bottle?"

He hated the woman who could only repeat what his grandfather said. He felt the eyes of the men at the bar on his skin. He took the bottle and filled the glass to the top.

"Good, Sebastian! Wash your sadness away! Sadness is good for nothing." After he had downed his third glass, Sebastian lifted his eyes, and looked at the men lined up at the bar. He noticed sympathy in their eyes. By then, he felt grown up, equal to everyone at the bar. He was no longer fourteen, but an indefinite age between twenty and thirty. He leaned against the bar and began drinking his fourth glass of wine.

"So, is this the visiting grandson?" said the woman. Sebastian's gaze drifted in the direction of her voice. The woman was washing dishes under the faucet. When she rubbed the glass, her arm muscles

flexed softly. She smiled at him and Sebastian discovered a new face replacing the hard one he had seen before. Now her face was much more delicate: sometime before she spent years and years behind the bar, that woman had been a pretty girl.

"This grandson of yours is a grown man, Grandpa Martin," added the woman, her lips moving as if they were butterflies. Sebastian tasted the sour flavor of the wine in his mouth, but the world held none of such sourness. On the contrary, the world became sweeter and sweeter. The grandfather was singing happily. The men talked to him with complete trust. The woman, that pretty girl in older days, moved gracefully behind the bar smiling at him each time she passed in front of him.

"Grandpa Martin knows how to talk to animals," he burst out suddenly. The words came up like hiccups, popping in his mouth like bubbles.

He regretted his words the moment he spoke them. Now the ten men at the bar looked at him as if he were a traitor, like when a visitor says something inappropriate. The song left his grandfather's lips and the woman's new smile showed something like pity or sadness. A husky man playing cards at the table broke the silence. "Sure, with animals like me; he talks to me sometimes!"

The whole bar exploded in loud laughter. The woman laughed too as she showed Sebastian a golden tooth. If earlier he had felt grown up, now he felt like a child. He went from fourteen to six.

"It's true, my grandpa . . ."

Sebastian wanted to tell them so many things, about his grandfather talking to the robin, scolding the snake. But the explanation seemed so hard. And besides, his tongue was in a knot, he could hardly move it.

"Take him home, Martin," said the woman. Without waiting for his grandfather's response, a man helped them get up from the chairs and took them to where Fangio waited peacefully. Both arrived at the aunt's house riding the donkey.

Sebastian's aunt had one leg which, from birth, was a little bit shorter than the other, and she limped a little when she walked fast. But Sebastian's father always said the limp wasn't the issue at all. The worst thing was how obsessed that woman was with her limp. Sebastian had that in mind when he saw her coming downstairs running.

"Aunt, you shouldn't let that limp bother you!"

But the aunt didn't pay any attention to the consolation. She ran straight to the grandfather.

"What, may I ask, have you been doing, Father? You got the boy drunk!"

The grandfather bowed his head, burying his chin in his chest. And remained there, even when the uncle took up the scolding where the aunt left off—sitting in the chair, mute, like clothing someone had discarded indifferently and left there. The wall's white tile, splashed with flies' droppings, made the grandfather's failing seem worse.

Sebastian was having a hard time comprehending what was going on in that kitchen. But he could sense the harshness of it: the aunt spoke breathlessly, the uncle waved his arms, filling the walls with dark shadows. The grandfather's silence begged for help.

"Grandpa knows how to talk to animals!"

"You poor thing," cried the aunt.

"Martin, you can't even take care of a kid!" shouted the uncle.

"Don't you see what a mess we have now?"

"Good Lord, good Lord," sighed the aunt. "If my sister finds out!"

"But it's true," Sebastian tried once more, "my grandpa knows how to talk to animals!" His voice sounded as if it belonged to someone else.

"Take the boy to bed!" decided the uncle.

The grandfather looked up and seemed to stare at the gypsy girl on the calendar hanging on the wall. But his eyes could see no further than the table and his gaze was lost there.

"Don't worry! I'll soon go to Terranova and I'll leave you in peace."

"Oh, Father! Don't you start in again with that Terranova story!"

"I'll leave soon, you'll see."

"Do you know where you are going? To bed!" ordered the uncle.

"But, Grandpa knows how to talk to animals!"

"You too, Sebastian, come with me to bed!"

The last time Sebastian looked at his grandfather, he was moving his lips as if he were praying. He only caught one word: Terranova.

That day their walks together ended. From then on, Sebastian had to go out to the plaza of Obaba all by himself.

The August sun, a full fifteen hours in the sky, dominated the whole town. It pushed people toward the darkness, and the coolness of the rooms was guarded inside the houses like a treasure. Only two kinds of beings stood the heat outdoors: cats and teenagers. Cats went to sleep, using up the very last inch of shade. The young people, less easy to satisfy, sought out the protection of the blue and white awning of the bar and drank cold lemonade mixed with beer to ease somewhat the sweaty burden of the heat.

Sebastian, likewise, had no other refuge; the benches in the plaza were sizzling and the banana trees with wide leaves were no match for the sun's assault. The awning afforded the only relief. And Sebastian began drinking the lemonade mixed with cold beer, alongside the unfamiliar youngsters of Obaba.

When night came and the temperature dropped, those young people, bored with sitting still, began to play games unknown to Sebastian.

"Let's play *fuego*!"

They made up two teams and each chose a bench in the plaza. The game lasted until one team got all of its players to the other bench. It was not easy, because once leaving the bench, trying to dash to the other side, the player could be taken prisoner. Every time someone was caught, the captor said *ble* and took the captive back to their side, leaving him there making the sign of the cross.

They never invited Sebastian to play with them, and he would spend the afternoon with his drink as his only company. Still, he did not leave the shade of that blue and white awning. He spent hours watching that battle in the plaza.

Although he had to suffer that loneliness, he did not miss the walks with his grandfather and a week was almost enough to completely forget the adventure with the bird and the snake on the day he got drunk.

But in order to understand Sebastian's behavior, it is necessary to say a few words about love.

When men and women turn fourteen, give or take a little, they experience a big inner change. Until then they scarcely have names. Well, they have names but they do not realize the difference that names mark and they live together with others and long to be like everyone else around them. They suffer, for instance, if their schoolmates ignore them, or if they cannot make friends in the neighborhood. But one day, their thoughts and desires take a hundred-and-eighty-degree turn. All at once, they are aware of their names; that no two are the same. Suddenly, they begin looking for a particular way to write their names. Finding a signature, a distinctive scribble, becomes the most important thing in life. The signature can take any shape, as long as it does not look like another in the world. In fact, they feel unique, and the scribbling with the pen must reflect that uniqueness.

Once they discover a signature, they feel like Robinson Crusoe. "What is the world?" they wonder, and come to the conclusion that it is an empty island. They have their whole lives to organize it, from the smallest detail to the biggest thing. And they do it all by themselves, through their own power. They make plans and, often with the help of a diary, they begin planning their future. What it will be like, what kind of a job they will have, where they would like to live.

Nevertheless, the solitude of fourteen-year-olds is just an illusion, a blinking light that goes on as it goes off. In the end, they have not been born to live in solitude; in the end, we all are more or less the same. And because of that, because that isolation is an illusion, fourteen-year-old youngsters fall in love.

One day boy meets girl and feels an explosion inside. From then on, as they say in Naples, *il primo amore* takes many forms. For some, it's like a warm wine that permeates their insides; for others, a feeling that brings the scent of grass or a flower. And there are also some that start seeing new colors when they fall in love. They see purple in the gray sky, see the woods as if made out of black marble, the roads, half-yellow, half-orange.

From the very first time she looked at him, Sebastian felt a combination of all those feelings for a lanky girl that played *fuego* in the plaza. Obaba seemed so colorful now. Where before he saw a normal street, he now saw a line of fire and golden roofs. The combination of beer and lemonade now tasted like strawberries. And on top of that, he constantly sensed the pungent smell of tomato plant leaves under the blue and white awning, and a few hours later when he lay on his bed.

Sebastian would spend the whole afternoon without rising from his chair. His only activity consisted of counting how many times she looked at him, to be written down later in his notebook.

August 9: Today she looked at me thirteen times.

August 13: Today only four times. She has gray eyes.

August 20: Twenty times!

August 22: I couldn't count them. She wore her hair differently.

August 24: I couldn't count them. Her name is Mariatxo. Her knees are round. Obaba smells like tomato leaves.

Sebastian ended up with every single day of his vacation planned in his notebook. In the morning, go out to try to see Mariatxo. In the afternoon, gaze at Mariatxo, and yearn for her glances. At night, think about Mariatxo, about her round knees and her slightly drooping lips.

He would see Grandfather Martin only at noon, but he hardly had a chance to talk to him. His aunt and uncle were always mad: "Father, why do you eat so much? Father, why do you eat so little?" The grandfather bowed his head and retaliated once more with his threat, "Don't worry! I'll go to Terranova soon!"

"Father, don't start with that again!"

It hurt Sebastian that his grandfather seemed more childish than he, and he tried to say something nice once in a while.

"But Grandpa, why do you want to go to Terranova? There's nothing but ice and coldness there!"

"And here? Isn't there ice and coldness here?" his grandfather would answer. Then he would fall silent, and his aunt would start crying. Then, his uncle would complain, murmuring to himself about their bad luck, and would look straight at Sebastian. The look bespoke: why do we have to have the old grandfather? Why not you, the city relatives? Isn't he your mother's father?

Sebastian decided to keep quiet and used lunch time to think about Mariatxo. In a few minutes, in the plaza, he was going to see the lanky girl who inspired all the words in his notebook. And that was enough for him.

After a month in Obaba, on the last day of August, Mariatxo came to the blue and white awning.

"Do you want to play *fuego*? We are one person short."

Sebastian faithfully transcribed the episode word for word in his notebook.

August 31. Mariatxo came to me and invited me to play with her. Everything went fine. I rescued her twice from prison. We won. Mariatxo, I love you. I think she feels the same about me, but I'm not sure.

The next entry, dated September 3, had something new: Today we didn't stay in the plaza, we went to the fountain. Mariatxo smells of tomato leaves. I

wrote home telling them I'll stay here one more month.

The entry from September the fifth was brief, but important: Today Mariatxo kissed me. Mariatxo, I love you.

The second week of September he started fulfilling the obligations of someone in love: he began telling her his secrets. He talked so much he did not know what to say on the seventh day. Mariatxo looked at the ground, and her legs, draped in blue and white socks, rotated in circles around an imaginary center. As sometimes happens to those in love, he was afraid Mariatxo would get bored, and his hands sweated heavily. As he was searching his memory for secrets, he found Grandpa Martin.

"My grandpa knows how to talk with animals, really." This time Mariatxo looked at him skeptically. She didn't laugh like the men at the bar, she did not scold him. But she did not show any curiosity like with the other secrets.

"You don't believe me?"

"Yes, but . . ."

Sebastian bravely argued his case: how the robin came making circles in the sky; how the snake surrendered; how the threatening dogs fell silent.

"But your grandpa, he's not very well, is he?"

"What do you mean?"

"They say he always talks about going to Terranova."

It seemed everybody in Obaba knew about Grandpa's plan. If Sebastian had still been a child he would not have been able to rebel, but in the nearly forty days he had spent in Obaba, he had crossed the invisible line between childhood and manhood and he decided to stand up for his grandpa:

"Well, if he says he's going, he'll go!"

"Maybe," said Mariatxo, her gray eyes turning serious. "Besides, people are foolish and they laugh at things they don't understand. Most people in Obaba don't even know where Terranova is."

Sebastian sensed the smell of tomato leaves more sharply than ever.

Peeking at the sky, he found the colors of the cardinal's winged cape, gold and purple. He decided that he would write a poem for Mariatxo.

He went to work that very same night. He wanted to include so many things in that poem: Mariatxo's gray eyes, her round knees, her white stockings, her voice, the scent of carnations (tomato leaves, of course, did not seem romantic enough), the sound of the fountain, summer, the game in the plaza, and a long etcetera of items that go hand in hand with love.

Since he wanted to make it short enough to be sent to her on a card, it was difficult to include all of those thoughts in the poem. He kept working until two in the morning. Then, only after he had finished, did he go to brush his teeth.

"And you, what are you doing here?"

Grandfather Martin stared at him seriously from the other side of the corridor.

"Grandpa, where are you coming from?"

"Who are you?"

"Me?"

"Yes, you!"

Sebastian realized that his grandfather had just come back from talking with the animals. Like three days after Sebastian arrived in Obaba, his grandson seemed a stranger.

"I'll help you to bed, Grandpa Martin."

Sebastian spent the whole night without being able to fall asleep; he was too busy thinking about the success he was going to have with Mariatxo the next day.

"It's incredible, Sebastian," she said. "It makes me a little scared."

"Tonight I'll stay awake, and if Grandpa leaves the house I'll follow him."

"But be careful, Sebastian."

"I will, Mariatxo."

As Sebastian had suspected, around midnight, his grandfather mounted Fangio and took the path toward the hills. The moon was full and the houses of Obaba seemed to be half-finished, an abandoned construction site, one missing a roof, the entire left side missing on another. A few of them had become merely doors and lighted windows, hanging in the air.

Sebastian followed his grandfather, and in fifteen minutes the night that had been completely silent filled with soft howls, cracking sounds, and far-off cries. When a dog barked, Sebastian felt relieved. At least he could recognize that noise. After half an hour on the trail, they had reached quite an altitude and

the lights of the village seemed like a dream. He knew Grandpa Martin had finished his trip. He left Fangio behind and he walked toward the woods.

There was a rocky area where the trail ended, and that's where Sebastian stopped. The grandfather, his lips murmuring that psalm-like melody, was hard at work, making little fires, like those made with matches. Later, in his notebook, Sebastian summarized what he saw on this day: September 17. Last night, I followed Grandpa to the woods. He made a few fires when he arrived there, and then, a few minutes later, a wild boar showed up, and then two more, then four or five more; they kept coming until the woods filled with wild boars. All the wild pigs went toward Grandpa. They did not look like wild boars, but behaved like dogs instead, wagging their tails and licking Grandpa's hand. Grandpa preached them a sermon and then they began snorting, the sound rising like thunder, and I wondered how people in town did not hear it. When I heard that rumble, I got a lump in my throat and a tremendous urge to cry came over me. It seemed like the wild boars were singing and it sounded like a church hymn. I could not stay there any longer, so I ran home and when I went to brush my teeth, I realized how pale I looked. But it was not from fear, it was something else.

"And the wild pigs licked his hand?"

"They did, Mariatxo!"

"But, why did you get so sad . . . after seeing that? Sebastian, you look so sad . . ."

"I don't know, I feel something here, deep inside."

Sebastian pointed at the spot between his chest and his stomach. Mariatxo, following her womanly instincts, embraced him.

On succeeding nights, Grandpa Martin talked to the brook trout and the village dogs and cats in the same fashion. Sebastian remembered two things from those spying sessions: how the trout had jumped for almost two hours and how the dogs had whimpered. And both memories made him sad, yet he did not know why.

September the twentieth was a special day in Obaba. It snowed in the hills, and swallows, thousands of them, perched in rows on the power lines. It seemed that winter had come earlier than ever before.

That night, Sebastian heard a knocking on his bedroom door. "Is that you, Grandpa?"

"Just a visit, a little visit."

"Yes, Grandpa."

Sebastian felt a bit ashamed, as do all young people who have heard the intimate secrets of someone older. His heart was split in two. He wanted to talk to his grandfather, but on the other hand he was afraid of what he might hear. That urge to cry tickled his throat. But his grandfather behaved normally, he seemed concerned with his grandson's affairs.

"Is everything going well with Mariatxo?"

"Yes, everything is very fine."

As best he could, struggling with his nervousness, Sebastian told his grandfather a few love secrets. How he met Mariatxo in the plaza, how she smelled of tomato leaves. But he also had a request.

"Grandpa, aren't you going to tell me anything about the animals?"

Grandpa Martin looked him straight in the eye.

"Didn't you see it, boy?" said the grandfather.

"Yes," admitted Sebastian lowering his eyes.

"Then . . . there's nothing else to tell, don't you think?"

"No."

He could not hold it in any longer and he began crying. He had just realized that Grandpa Martin was telling him goodbye, saying a last farewell just as he did with the wild boars, trout, dogs, and cats. The grandfather joked as he was leaving, "And you, boy, what are you doing here?" and he laughed as if telling Sebastian to cheer up. And lowering his voice, "Take care, Sebastian."

"Bye, Grandpa."

The next day it drizzled from daybreak. The world was totally quiet: the crickets under the earth, the swallows on the wires, the chained dogs in front of the houses, all were silent. At five in the afternoon, as they stood at the fountain, Mariatxo turned Sebastian's attention to the sky.

"Geese, Sebastian."

Geese head toward the warmth of the coast as soon as they sense winter coming, making letters with their flight formations. That is why they say that heaven writes through the geese. And Mariatxo knew that.

"They've made a B."

Those that passed by at a quarter past five made a Y. Those passing at five-thirty made an E. Between the three of them, they made a farewell word: BYE.

"The next group is going to make an M," said Sebastian. But this time there were three groups in a row: MAR. Then, a T went flying by. Around seven, the last ones wrote IN.

The geese wrote, "BYE MARTIN." "Grandpa must have gone to Terranova." Sebastian was in no hurry. Taking slow steps, he headed toward his aunt's house. When he was near, he could see the commotion around it. There were many people gathered by the entrance and his uncle was showing them a piece of paper. "I have gone to Terranova," it said.

A little later, some men brought Fangio home, saying that the old man was nowhere to be found.